Even in the
Slums of Providence

poems by

Larry Pike

Finishing Line Press
Georgetown, Kentucky

Even in the
Slums of Providence

For Carol,
Daniel and David.

In memory of Joy Bale Boone—
true poet, true friend.

Publisher: Leah Huete de Maines
Editor: Christen Kincaid
Cover Art: Shelby Bale, oil-on-canvas painting called "Here I Am"
Author Photo: Bryn Chapman
Cover Design: Elizabeth Maines McCleavy

Order online: www.finishinglinepress.com
also available on amazon.com

Author inquiries and mail orders:
Finishing Line Press
P. O. Box 1626
Georgetown, Kentucky 40324
U. S. A.

Table of Contents

3. LUXURIES THAT EXCEED OUR GRACE

1.

SHOULD HAVE HELD OUT
FOR MORE WATER

In the Driveway

Puffs of breath whisper
the morning's temperature.
My mother, on the porch gripping
an awning post, considers how
I secure the last items
in my car. I assure my father
I checked the oil, nod
at where he tells me to get
cheap gas. There's nothing left
to do, the long drive,
and all. A glance back to say
yes, I'll be careful,
and I see something

I don't remember. Dad,
still in his slippers, is smaller,
Mom favors a withered leg.
They lean together. I am
grayer than they were
when I became a man. I am
older yet when we acknowledge
the moment. Hasty waves,
some self-conscious sentences
clutter the gleaming air
like late leaves lifted
from the branches of one tree,
then another.

My EKG

Of course it's precautionary, probably
will be discontinued once the echo
results are back, but being handed
the nitro scrip jolts the pulse,
stimulates sharp, darting pains,
which would seem contraindicated.
I feel a searing sensation accompanying
the removal of tapes securing sensors to my chest,
where I finger a suddenly smooth spot,
considering a future that feels
like someone else's, tastes
fleeting under my tongue.

Common Stock

My speakerphone broadcasts
the 2nd conference call today,
5th this week. On MUTE

my co-conspirators don't
hear me checking my e-mail, scrolling
through another tedious corporate directive,

munching an onion bagel, chatting quickly
with a colleague who needs a P.O. OK'd.
This call is a pep talk, a prayer offered to troops

about to wade onto the beach. In an hour,
tomorrow, or early next week,
my teleconferees and I will sit face-to-face

with some fellow employees. We'll tell
our human resources their jobs can't be
justified, based on benchmarked ratios.

We'll tell them about earnings pressures
intensified by the softening economy
and a sluggish demand for services.

It's all cost vs. value,
we'll say, nothing
personal—which is, of course, the most personal thing

we can say. We won't blame a calculating executive,
who misses the irony when he gazes at the photo
of his three kids playing on a less dangerous beach,

for approving their terminations.
And we won't admit
we recommended them.

Happy Hour with Bill

Over appetizers your memory smoked
with aromas of everything we burned decades ago:
gas, rubber, midnight oil, bridges between girls we chased
and their fathers, most of whom had the good sense
to let their daughters have nothing to do with us.
They filled our nostrils like intoxicating vapors,
volatile compounds in the presence of excitable genes,

and we skittered after them all over our neighborhoods—
Lucy, Laurie, Jackie, Paula, Phyllis and Nancy,
and Andrea or Amanda, I forget which.
We were as predictable as I remember, no matter what
you say, a few beers don't improve that.
Me? I had a thing for your sister, who liked movies
and pizza, and I was as up for that as the next guy.

Hard Hat

A tired candy bar suffered a heat stroke
during the first week of summer,
and slumped over the fingers of a burly
steel worker who had something tattooed
in Chinese across the knuckles of his left hand.

"*Shee*-it," he muttered, and wiped
the chocolate mess on his t-shirted chest,
a hole, pretending to be a navel, visible
in the middle of a basketball stomach.
"You have a helluva time running

this canteen, don't ya?" He spoke at me
with a rumbly voice that swelled
from his throat, mucus-covered.
"So damn many people around all the time.
Hell's bells!" Burly informed me and my

eighteen vending machines, eleven humming
softly, keeping something hot or cold,
or just kept. Before I could answer,
he picked up his coffee, spilling half
on his tattooed hand with a lively curse,

and hardly looking from beneath hooded lids,
found his way back into June and the dust
to the third splice, one hundred twenty-six feet up.
To hell with something,
he didn't say what.

There's Something Happening Here

According to the whispers of well-meaning friends,
my wife has been seen around town
with a paunchy, graying guy who may
or may not walk sometimes with a slight limp.
One neighbor predicts, on the strength of medical records
training, a hip replacement or perhaps a 'scope of a knee,
and says the fellow would be about my height
if he didn't stoop. We have similar features,
except for the heavy circles under his eyes. Unlike me,
he allegedly works too much and plays too little,
doesn't always pay attention, and leaves the seat up.
He claims he doesn't snore, color-coordinates only with khaki,
can't hit a 4-iron, and nods off in front of the TV in prime time.
Maybe I'm missing something. I don't understand the attraction.
But I'm taking all this in, I'm not just sitting back on the couch.
I've shuffled around the block. I'm thinking about trying
a different haircut or a temporary tattoo,
buying a crisp new dress shirt, switching to soft spikes,
and eating more Mexican food—I can tolerate hot salsa,
don't let anyone say I can't, and two margaritas, maybe,
if I don't drive. I might have to consider formulating
a new contingency plan as the backup plan
for my fallback plan, the plan I am already working on.

Comet

A hundred times I've studied the newspaper
photograph since the sordid trial of a reckless
but not uncommon man. In it he is no longer free,
already handcuffed to an unimagined future.

His mother clings to his neck, his father grips
the shoulder of a boy he can no longer help.
They will go to their graves with this,
having anguished over what they did,

and unable to divine error in lenience or discipline,
will despair at having done nothing else instead.
One's child is always a child to love, worry over,
encourage, and cry for, but time and opportunity

pass swiftly, uneasy lessons too often wisps
in an expanding universe. Parenthood is its own prison,
a general population of self-doubts, second-guesses,
recriminations, mounting evidence, appeals and appeals,

verdicts open to question. You do the next thing
you can see to do. And hope and hope and hope.
That is all I know—and this: I did my best very early
one Sunday in February 1986. I woke my six-year-old,

helped him dress quickly in the dark, eased us quietly
from the house. We drove to a chilly knob, sat on
the hood of the car, arms hugged into coat sleeves. Once
in a lifetime we scanned the sky for Halley's icy apparition.

Maybe a miracle will allow us to conduct this search
together again, so does it really matter that we couldn't find
the fluorescent coma, the dusty tail pressed across space?
And who can say we didn't?

My Father's Socks

In the nightstand drawer they might be still
balled, soft knots, patternless
over-the-calf navy, black, and brown
matches for the fine midnight blue wool,
supple glen plaid, and crisp khaki

suits of the year my dad and I wore
the same size—maybe the longest
twelve months of his life, he'll tell you.
Slipping into my father's clothes made me
wiser, I thought, as I swept back the jacket,

affecting a worldly hands-in-pockets pose,
the attitude needed to ponder a project,
assess an opportunity, decide on a deal.
Years later, I applied the lessons learned
in my father's socks. I bought dull

old-man duds, gambling my own boys wouldn't
find them appealing when our sizes converged.
Yet my older son always got first to the shirt
I planned to wear to work, my younger son
to the pair of socks not already thin at the heel.

To a Little Girl Considering a Snapping Turtle on Spring Branch

A plodding approach doesn't always mean
there's no plan. Ask the hare.
This is a turtle. It is not
the lazy box that trudged up from the creek
and baked on wide summer asphalt.
It is definitely not one of the cute
painted miniatures trolling pet shop terrariums.
See how it idles in the marsh?
It can't catch, so it doesn't chase; instead it watches,
and waits. It shares sluggishness with its cousins, but enjoys
a nasty disposition all its own. Evolved (or not)
as a pitiable rocklike creature, it invites you: *Come
closer, touch here.* Tap the spiny shell,
rap the tormented existence,
its head snaps out, its only quick condition.
Reach out. Your itchy fingers
skitter like lizards, little toes twitch like grubs.
Jaws like blades will bite, break flesh
and maybe bone; blood will bubble. Almost every time.
The lesson is in the luring

you shouldn't answer. This caution
will make sense tomorrow or some day after,
when you're long past wandering along the mud bank,
when your curiosity has shifted
from what swims in the stream's slow swirls
to shifty older boys (who may yet evolve),
smooth and strong and slick,
trolling patiently through the neighborhood, watching,
inviting you: *Come closer, reach out,*
and your mother gives you another stern warning
about predatory reptiles lying low in tall grass.

A Matter of Public Record

No secret why you're here, you
know. Shafts of light angle across
the mess hall floor. Thousands of steps

shift down the food line,
millions of furtive eyes measure
bland portions spooned onto chipped trays.

No mystery, really, to the three hots,
one about like another, the sameness
one less pressure. The calculations, though,

never total, always scores to figure, something
always to be settled, bartered, hoarded
against some future enterprise, a reality show

that never ends. You never know.
A price has to be paid, a debt to society,
whatever it may be. You remind yourself

you're not here for crimes committed.
If what they charged you with was all they had,
you'll take the weight. It's time, is all.

This mess? You've seen it: coming in
from a road crew, marching down
the tiers at a federal pen, hanging around

a sixth-floor window, standing on one leg
on a box on the other side of the world, scrambling
eggs in a kitchen in a low-rent walkup, carrying

a chipped tray to a table in a cinder-block
corporate cafeteria in an industrial park
beside an expressway going nowhere fast.

No secret why you're here. The calculations,
the daily commute, the details, the crimes
not yet committed, the ones not yet imagined.

Hippos Humping

—for those on Capitol Hill

My dirty little secret?
I like to watch.
Real sex acts! Secret love tapes!
on cable-ready educational TV,
captured by a video crew
with a government grant.

A tight two-shot:
great gray hippos, slick
with mud and primal musk,
cooperating in heat rising from heat,
huge male behind female—
someone's son, someone's daughter—
nature's favorite waltz, slow dance performed
with the heft and sway of armored cars.

Cut to a wide shot in naked light.
The camera's impolite stare embarrasses
the bull's putative bride. She waddles
into the brush, a discreet score to settle.
Her surprisingly nimble suitor,
not to come undone,
trots in synchrony behind her
in the consensual privacy of my home.

Thank God for our famous freedoms,
assembly and the press.
All congressional acts should be so
bipartisan.

Statues in an Antique Store

Anyone could have confronted the startling pair
in the fusty shop entrance. Today, I shouldered open
the swollen door, escaping the swelter, and faced
a raised spear, looked from one panting mouth to another,
but no sharp jab or hot breath backed me over the jamb.

The diminutive native and his mate were fine objects
conceived by a masterful artist who chipped and shaved
precise musculature from seasoned logs, hand-rubbed
trunks and limbs until the dark patina of jungle flesh
glistened in the humidity of a darker world. I shrank

from the anguish shaped in their faces. I turned my head
to glimpse the threat. What was there to see?
The brave male defending his hut or driving some foe
into dense growth? The woman restraining her husband
or propelling him toward danger? I circled the figures for clues

in the clever flex of arms, nimble balance of weight on legs.
Only two things were revealed in the sculptor's installation.
The moment's urgency surpassed my ordinary experiences—
going to work, mowing the lawn. And everything
you've heard about the aphrodisiac of fear is true,

obvious in the frightened woman's tight nipples
and under the hunter's loincloth, deftly shaped along
a warp of bark to appear to be lifted by a sudden gust.
Even an apprentice carver could see it for what it was:
the absolute representation of wood.

Tasseled Loafers

Last week I heard on NPR a retired men's store owner
lament the current style with which I've grown comfortable.
He advocated a return to certain sartorial traditions,
a dignity observable even on radio, so I listened

to his arguments opposing casual Fridays and other
crimes against fine fabric. He could have been one
of the tailors, tape measure draped around his neck
like a stethoscope, who welcomed gentlemen and their sons

at the downtown clothier where my father took me
to be fitted for the tasseled loafers all my friends wore,
handsewn calfskins with a wide toe box and narrow heel
that slid onto the feet and flexed with a limber hinge.

To enter the Shoe Room, we'd stride the length of the store,
past slacks terraced like Incan hillsides on broad oak
tables, past over-and-under racks of conservative suits,
mid-weight worsteds with a smooth hand, busy fellows

intent on an important mission—but not too hurried
for my dad to speak with the men he knew, those
who had knelt to chalk a cuff for the right shoetop break,
selected ties he always appreciated as what he had in mind.

The Camel's Back

More and more I'm the oldest guy
out there, except when my friend Joe
joins the neighbors chatting

in a knot under the streetlight.
The shifting shadows make it difficult,
sometimes, to see the elderly beagle crawl

through the hedge, showing off
the smooth ratchet of the artificial hip
I envy. I follow his smug waddle

away from the crescendo of gossip that falls
short of my good ear. I decide this
four-legged beneficiary of veterinary technology—

this is the last straw. I am not a dog person.
Yet he stops me in my own tracks when he turns
and shares with me a weary, empathetic look.

He knows his titanium-and-plastic days are numbered.
The last straw is the one that enjoys a certain celebrity,
gets video at eleven. But the first straw—

that little bastard travels the backroads, incognito,
sneaks into town to stir up some trouble,
leaves with no forwarding address.

Cycle

This little desire settled on me earlier today,
in traffic, while I was caught at a light. A big bike
glided to a stop in the turn lane next to me.
A man in sunglasses balanced the ride on

steady feet familiar with its weight. Behind him
a pretty woman knotted a thick ponytail, laughing
at something I didn't quite hear, straight teeth bright
in the glare. The guy nodded, rolling the throttle

absently with a practiced hand while she rocked
her boots on the pegs, hooked her thumbs
at the waist of her faded, faded jeans, so close
I could almost stroke the soft finish of denim

not as blue as the clear sky, but blue enough.
I had to glance away from the curve of her hip.
Their signal changed. The man released the clutch
as the woman fanned a few sandy strands wisping

about her face. She lurched with the acceleration,
breasts rising against the close knit of her shirt.
Leaning into the turn away from me, she hugged
herself firmly into him. Not that I minded

my quick run for milk and bread, a helpful task I do
as easily as the biker shifted gears, but there are times,
that moment on the street, perhaps, when I might
wish to have that guy's back, feel that grip in my chest.

Mourners Leaned Against Their Cars

—for Martha

> *Coronavirus restrictions prohibit mass gatherings,*
> *impact funeral attendance (April 2020).*

A sparse crowd wasn't the graveside service
my friend's father wanted after ninety-three years.
Another viral insult, a smattering of mourners

leaned against their cars, squatted on headstones
or shifted in open grass safely distant from the family.
Colorful masks protected faces nodding sympathies

in lieu of handshakes and hugs, oddly unsatisfying
remembrances. Sounds of road repair blocks away
interrupted recordings of hymns. A rooster's alert

quavered on gusts that fluttered dewy branches
and carried few of the minister's words. Perhaps
just as well. Some might say this was a sign.

Instead of a splendid throwdown, the old codger got
let down by the handful scattered across the grounds.
The preacher assured everyone the deceased knew

where he was going in the next life—fair consolation,
I believe, for this life being so unpredictable, clever
mischief throughout, bait-and-switch at the end.

Tipping Point

That frigid Saturday midnight
my mother's car rolled
out of the garage
after me because I failed
to park four wheels
on the plane of cement
then compounded my error
by leaving it in neutral
and not pulling the hand brake
I learned much
more about physics
than from all the deadly
high school lectures
I had dozed through
though Mr. Stanfield
would've been fascinated
by how nimbly I grasped
concepts of gravity and
equilibrium and mass
and escape velocity
the moment before
I braced
one hand and foot
against fifty-year-old brick
and the other on
the approaching icy steel
trunk and bumper
to save the house
and my bones
only to have
my bravura flattened
when I plucked
woody shreds
from the undercarriage
and had to concede
gnarly branches
of frost-burned shrub

had seized
a passing axle
and arrested
the fugitive compact
before a crushing impact
and the last time
I was home
those limbs still jutted
in the cold dark
like my dad's arms
while his voice rose
as blood beat
in his ears
wondering
just what I had done
this time.

Dream House

Last night at our favorite Mexican place,
dinner and conversation progressed
with practiced ease. We rarely dipped
tortilla chips in salsa at the same time,

I let you finish most of your sentences,
you pushed the grilled onions to me.
The warmth and sweetness weren't
all margarita and flan. I imagined

their momentum might last until we got home,
that other appetites might be satisfied.
In the bedroom you fiddled
with the remote, finding your channel.

I slipped behind you, cupped my hands
at your waist, nuzzled your neck.
You hip-checked me away. When we crawled
under the covers it was just to watch

a young couple with expensive tastes quibble
over fancy homes in South Florida suburbs.
He wanted ocean access, she wanted something
with a white kitchen close to her parents.

By the time they settled on a foreclosure
in Mommy and Daddy's neighborhood
that had dark granite countertops
and backed up to a manmade lake,

you were already sound asleep.
Waiting for the next show, I pulled
the comforter tight under my chin and thought
the guy should have held out for more water.

2.

SOLVED FOR *X* INSTEAD OF *Y*

At the Game Preserve

A crippled buck wanders an enclosure,
alert to generous visitors who
poke through chain link
shoots of grass, wildflowers, offerings
more appealing than the hay
bunk filled every day along
the tall fence line of habitat
he'll never appreciate as protective.

He maintains a counterclockwise graze
dictated by the lost left eye,
a sentry patrolling a worn perimeter
described by a relentless list,
right shoulder and haunch bulked
by the perpetual push to see
what is always just around the bend,
the haughty curvature of his earth.

Most times his sideways stare fixes on
the unseeing, those clinging at the wire
who comment on his damaged rack,
that smudge of socket, those who wonder what
he thinks about, who don't hear me say,
Open forest, which doesn't take two
good eyes to remember, those who do hear me
say, *Keeping the wild world in sight.*

Before Mammoth Cave

Go on. Go. Between preparation and hesitation
there is enough space:
squeeze through.

Small sneaky stones beneath
loose leaves will make you slip
sooner than anything you see

ahead. Whatever's clear you can make wider
if you're not too careful about your steps.
Go on: you'll stand at last

in chilly mist spreading from the splash
spilling through fern and moss over the rock
at the beginning of the world. Reach

there: you can capture a few drops
and wash your face
with that vivid water.

Sitting Behind Seven Women

They're two, maybe three, sets of sisters,
a group four rows ahead of me,
a holiday-week afternoon outing,
time for friends to do nothing well. A movie,

then dinner, white zinfandel and grilled chicken;
one will finally order crème brulee,
another, tiramisu—with two spoons—
something sly shared. Soft chatter

over the previews, prequel to quiet
laughter, absent toss of one's hair,
brush of downy pinfeather from another's jacket.
How well they know each other reveals itself

more clearly than the screenplay's storyline.
They team-teach at the same middle school, work
on the same floor at the bank downtown,
carpool to grad school, and even the little sisters

volunteer as Big Sisters, women I could know—
my older son's landlord, the friend who lives
in the little house on the hill, an x-ray technician
or marketing assistant, a used book shop manager.

When I crinkle the candy wrapper in my coat pocket,
when I crunch chips of ice from my drink cup,
the younger brunette who reminds me of how
my wife looked to me years ago

turns her head quickly in my direction,
her brow slightly arched,
a glance that reminds me of how
my wife sometimes looks at me today.

Flow

If you can sing, then you can dance,
my best friend's older sister tried to
tell me, her seductive harmony coaxing
scratchy 45s from the turntable's stack,
her gracious ear deaf to my desperate tones,

thick hair swirling about her face like her hips
whirled across her bedroom floor.
I'll remember the songs if I can only think
as hard as I wanted to believe in her
motion, super-colliding particles racing

around a molten nucleus, scorching the air.
She pulled at my hands, jerky swim-and-pony
movements mirrored, but my shy shuffle stopped
when she canceled the touch, our circuit broken,
my timid soul a poor conductor for her energy:

heat or light, but not both.

My Albanian Nurse

Bruna, RN, BSN, swept into South 389
with the efficiency expected of her
lavender scrubs and stiff white cap.

She received the attention demanded by her
flawless complexion and shiny dark hair.
The morphine drip was no match for the Adriatic

air that breezed about my hospital room.
When she positioned the cool stethoscope
near a lapro puncture, when she touched

my tender belly with her fingertips, when
she whispered, "Let me listen to you,"
there was no limit to the lies I was prepared to tell.

Near the Border

—for Petie

Let's call the girl in the photograph Rosa or Maria
—bright names that go with her eyes. See,
something playful occupied her attention

across the pale room, her slight smile unintended
for the camera, unaware of aperture, shutter and flash.
Her image was last held under mesquite cover,

tilted toward campfire and starlight just so
that sweet face could be seen again
before the *coyotes** arrived. In the scramble

for space in an airless truck that barely slowed,
her picture fluttered unclutched to the dust
among scattered packs, empty water jugs, clothes

abandoned with no thought for such small hope,
an unlikely deliverance. Somewhere in the desert
during the desperate ride from hell

someone patted a breast pocket, and felt
instead of the creased, glossy paper
only her memory.

---

* Human smugglers who guide illegal immigrants across the desert for a fee.

Down Home

I didn't know about building things then.
No way I thought your weary shack—tar paper
and sun-dried boards beaten like your ancestors'

backs over crumbly piers—should stand.
A wind half as hard as the baked
Georgia clay ought to have pushed it

beyond equilibrium. Its mean balance poised
on a fault line shifting under every generation
yet sturdy as the civil history

that spun our worlds in different planes:
great-great-grandsons of slave-owner and slave,
grandsons of poor farmer and poorer sharecropper,

sons of a spiteful South stringing us up,
suspending us over time in a place still as wicked
and mysterious as the physics of construction.

The Night Room

I have been in this room before,
one like it, one of a thousand, a million—
past the gift shop, the snack bar, x-ray, PT,
round and around the maze of wings,
2 East, 3 West, halfway down a hallway—

adjustable bed, leather-like recliner, mini-TV,
compact metal nightstand, rollaway tray;
vague blue paint on block; small shaded window
with a view, if you could move your head,
raise your eyes a little. I will watch

for you, the anticipated meteor shower tonight,
the drizzle forecast for later in the week.
This is what we've come to in this room: I wait,
thumbing last week's *Time* lifted from the lobby;
you consume tireless mechanical breaths.

Once, after you underwent a minor procedure,
we spent an uneasy night in a room like this. Sleepless,
I stood by you. In the vapor, snow dusted firs
along the parking lot I could see through the small window.
Each time you stirred against some pain, you asked

if I wasn't hungry, if I wasn't tired, didn't I want to go home.
You said, I'll be all right, I'll be right here,
do what you want. What I want now won't be satisfied
by a reflexive flutter of eyelids, subconscious
reply to this repeated plea: wake and tell me again.

I don't expect it. We wear a hopeless silence,
an unrepentant habit, something sterile
and sharp like the starched sheets changed
every day. A nurse rolls you, rocks you
back and forth, an empty ship drifting on a receding sea.

Dying

One Saturday afternoon, though there's no big rush,
you drive through your best college friend's hometown,
and don't stop to call. Soon after, you're too busy
to travel at Thanksgiving, and Christmas always comes

at a bad time, the year-end reports, a head start on January
projects, something somebody wants. Before long,
you've gone from listening to your parents rave about
the great deal they got on colonoscopies to swapping stories

with your dad about prostate biopsies, and you know
even before you know you know it—you've accelerated
your own certain decline. You understand
there will be a morning when your wife will leave

for work, the store, church, some life
you won't know she still has. You won't remember
if you waved good-bye. You'll look up from the comics,
wondering, "Was anyone here?"

In Memoriam

Jim died Sunday in a distant state, following
the familiar long illness. A colleague I saw once
every year or so, shared occasional phone calls with,

copied on periodic e-mails, I called him a friend.
I didn't know he had three kids, played
college football, or enjoyed sci-fi.

He was a couple of years younger, and got
tricked by an inadequate gene, but there was
a lot about him I didn't know, never

bothered to ask. It is a sorry eulogy.
What retirement plans did he have,
what did he still hope to accomplish,

was the light fragrance of time still about
his face when he last inhaled?
Would he have been interested to know

I once took flying lessons,
tried to learn to play the banjo,
wrote twenty-six pages of a novel?

Jim died Sunday in a distant, dismal place,
not far from the estate that waits for me,
a few yards of sod tamped over last light.

Faith

Outside the funeral home again
one afternoon last week I breathed
like I'd never tasted air. This time
it was a gun shot, or a car crash, a little fear

and neglect, a failed surgery, a bad age, a bad time,
or a bad decision—choose a reason for the residue,
the remains, the retinue in the weary line. In the end
the hand of God plays over the earth,

passing all the storied understanding;
it nudges and plucks, rights
some of what has fallen. I've reached
the awkward age: my curiosity doesn't always get

the best of me. I may not raise my hand,
and though I am making a neat list
in a precise script, I'm not worried. I'm not
worried. I can hold my questions for another time.

Work

Some people, left
to their own devices,
will do useful things—
like Phil the furnace
repairman who replaced
the sticky switch.

Melvin the mechanic
ID'd the cause
of the abrasive whistle,
and installed the brake pads
that kept Carol's car
off Bob's bumper.

Drywall Dennis
patched the blistered
ceiling so smoothly
that Sarah couldn't
tell the tile
shower ever leaked.

All this while Loophole Larry,
backpaddling at the
confluence of subject
and verb, parsed a paragraph
that Emily the employee might
interpret one way

and Stu her supervisor another—
this may be the point
of some devices, and people:
they should not be
left alone. When they are
you find what Terrell

the tree farmer found when,
in the winter wind,
he trudged up
from his village.
Wandering among his woods
he heard a whisper

of harness bells and
discovered, stamping at
the frost, a restless
one-trick pony, having
thrown its rider, clearly
miles and miles from home.

Tool

The walker stands
folded against the wall,
convenient to the chair

in which my mother
has fallen asleep,
a rest from her MS.

An elemental machine,
it's a veritable quantum leap
from crutch and cane's

simple aesthetics—
brushed aluminum nicked and dented,
tattoos of close encounters,

molded handgrips smoothed
by the repeated application of pressure
insistent as any natural force.

Its deceptive functionality
collapses the staggering distance
between points A and B,

adapting to the perilous surface
tension with a steadying effect
that mitigates the complex damage

of one foot's right-angle splay,
the ruin of one leg's
wheel and hinge.

My Broken Heart

—for Carol

No clinical assessment of arterial damage,
delivered moments after
the cath, prepares you, immobile
on a gurney under a twist of stiff sheet
and thin blanket, for a revelation
much less imagined than blockage.
Forbidden to raise even your head
over your objections, to avoid expelling
the femoral plug, your wife has
to help you pee. Familiar but unseen

fingers locate the receptacle, aim, drain
your puny bravado. The circumstantial
gravity is wrong, the mechanics untuned,
the gown lifted because it has to be, a curtain
hiding a dependency that defeats what
dignity we pretend. Sooner,
not later, what remains but
the hand we offer, the hand
we accept, the hand that greets
our mortality?

Called Out

—for Jeff Bruce

Really, I was pretty much settled in.
If Jesus had gotten here a day later
I might just have said, "No, thanks,
I'm good." That could have raised a stink,

but Martha would have shut up
for once, seen things someone else's way.
It's a lot of pressure, coming back—
tourists always staring; paparazzi

dogging my dusty walk to town; my favorite
bar a drag because on the next stool
there's some local toad who believes
he can be the one to put me down for good.

What can I say that doesn't sound
ungrateful? Not that I ever wanted to leave,
but neither did I expect a mulligan,
another chance to repair something

I didn't know I'd ruined, one more chance
to mend what had seemed unmarked
a year ago, last month, only days earlier.
It was quiet behind the stone. Soon, I'm afraid,

Mary may find me wandering, wary of my place
on this earth. She'll run to tell what she's seen,
smudges where I wiped my eyes with dirty hands,
and this is the word that will get around:

Lazarus wept.

Wedding Party

Casual grips on longnecks,
fast, loose dances,
delights among merry friends—
promise of youth rising like light
fog hovering nearby over cool grass.
Let them have this.
Nothing tonight will
linger. Soon enough
bride and groom will know
a distant vantage, hold tighter to

their claim to love. Unable to stop
themselves, in middle age
they'll raise like tonight's toasts
questions that will hang
dense and damp on their bones,
loll longer on their lips than this
evening's laughter. *Did we live?*
At least not waste much of what life
we had? Their quiet answers will be
little light in another fog.

This Afternoon in London

I stood in the museum's Reading Room
long enough to hear the grave whisper
of the gimpy Lord's soul as it pressed
against the leaded glass. Was it an alien

tongue or simply muffled sound indistinct
about my ear? Its swelling sigh did not arouse
the sentry who spared an indifferent look
at me leaning across the restraining rope,

my shadow spreading over the heavy pane
preserving Byron's frail pages—there and
there and there where I could not discern
his rapid hand on the brittle sheets.

The chill casement received my reckless touch
like a busy confessor eager for some original sin,
and discharged a meager static spark
through the window on the dead.

Easing Out the Clutch

—after Michael Pettit

Mom signaled, though no one followed our little car,
and turned into the big Baptist church's parking lot,
freshly sealed but not yet restriped, where she drifted

to the center of a black hole of asphalt, shifted
into neutral, tapped the brakes once or twice,
and stopped. I considered her from the passenger's side

as she set the hand brake and said, opening her door
and stepping out, "Switch places." I didn't move
as she curved around the bumper to stand beside me,

waiting for me to surrender my seat, saying nothing else,
demonstrating not so much patience as resolve, until
I hunkered past, circling to the other side. Wanting to drive

and wanting to learn to drive are different urges. Mom could
put me behind the wheel but she couldn't make me ease out
the clutch gently until I could sense the engine surge.

"Give it gas, but not so much at once, you'll feel it in your feet,"
she coached, then shut up and sat back. My pulse accelerated.
In her place Dad would have kept instructing, micromanaging,

expecting a fluid transfer of energy, a smoother roll
across the expanding pavement. I would have learned more
from him than how to drive—mechanics of the differential,

thermodynamics of internal combustion—maybe valuable
info for later. Mom just had me try. Of course
I stalled and bucked, but soon we were maneuvering

through suddenly open frontier down Friendly past Ham's
to West Greenway on wide whitewalls in the boxy Fiat 1100,
four doors, four on the tree, forever a ground gear from freedom.

Burned

—*after Anne Ross Bruce*

Then Abraham returned to his servants,
and they set off together....
—Genesis 22:19 (NIV)

Young Isaac had seen enough sacrifices to know
something was off—the long journey to a far mountain,
the confusing absence of a lamb. "God will provide, my son,"
Abraham said, an incomplete truth Isaac didn't recognize
until ropes were knotted and he was trembling on the wood.

Years later Isaac may have wondered why he couldn't protest
when Abraham bound him, why he looked up when Abraham
raised the knife, squinted against a beam bright as the image
of the Lord mirrored in the blade, and simply whispered, "Father?"
Everyone knows Abraham didn't open his son's throat

or burn his tender frame on the bitter altar. Everyone knows
an angel interceded, a ram appeared, trapped in a thicket.
Isaac survived. But say the angel had been delayed in traffic,
the ram had wriggled free, and Abraham, receiving no reprieve,
had plunged the knife and lit the flame. Back home,

what account could have satisfied Sarah? Everyone knows
crazy people say *God made me do it*. Sure,
God tested Abraham, and Abraham solved for *x* instead of *y*,
gambled on obedience rather than love. Maybe
God didn't mean to see if Abraham would give up

his treasure, but whether Abraham could stand up and say,
"Lord, no, You know this is wrong. Everyone knows."
After, Abraham loved Isaac, of course, likely with some guilt,
as fathers often do. He gave Isaac everything. Yet
at the end of his long life perhaps Abraham,

instead of never doubting his devotion, suffered some shame
that he hadn't raised a question instead of a knife;
recalled in his waning hours the complicated conversation
with Isaac as they watched the ram's charred bones cool;
regretted with his final breath descending the mountain alone

while Isaac remained, determined to have his own talk with God.

3.

LUXURIES THAT EXCEED OUR GRACE

Juleps on the Reading Porch

—for George Boone

Years before the Mexican
silversmith tooled the tall cups
favored for their quick and smooth frost,
the genteel process had been rendered.
Equal parts recipe and presentation,
the linen cloth vital
as the finely shaved ice,
the swollen wooden pestle no more
important than the mint just minutes
out of its garden spot by the side wall.
We sip through silver straws,
savoring the delicious scandal about
the ambassador's china, watching
with heavy lids as the women ride
the long arc of the rope swing,
skirts rising with the notes of
their laughter. We do not hurry.
Honeyed bourbon slips down our throats.
Breezes slide across our brows.
The day seeps away.

Photo from My Sister's Wedding

Mama kept the brittle Kodacolor print,
a glossy crosscut square, among her keepsakes
because it was the closest I got to marriage,

a junior bridesmaid in June 1952,
ankle-length taffeta, ribboned spray of pink
roses in white-gloved hands, long curls

ready to droop in the damp afternoon, when
Granddaddy snapped me, slightly smirking,
alone in the side yard off the wide porch.

I was fair then, ten-years-old, and starving,
as I recall. Inside the big house Memaw
and Aunt Clare fussed over Jean Ann,

twice my age, cinching her into all that lace,
and wouldn't let me eat, afraid I'd spot my dress.
Instead, Granddaddy said, "Buck up, Pumpkin,

you look right pretty," promising me cake
as soon as Jean Ann and Bo, who always
pressed between my shoulders a frosty Nehi

whenever I wandered by and forgot to twist away,
had claimed the first slice, smeared icing on their noses.
True as ever, Granddaddy brought me a plate,

and I licked every crumb from it. A lot has passed since,
including Jean Ann and Bo, Granddaddy, and Mama, too,
who never quit believing Mr. Right would come along

for me—or Ms. Right, I might say now, but not then,
we weren't that sort of mid-century modern.
That day wasn't the last time I'd get reminded

to deal with something or let it go, nowhere
near the last time I wouldn't sidestep quickly enough
to avoid a cold, unwanted touch, but it was when

I learned *pretty is as pretty does*, a kind of bucking up
you could say, and now and again a pang blooms
low in my belly, every now and again it surely does.

To My Older Son, Soon to Marry

Once or twice a month, while on my way
somewhere else, I drive by the house
where you were conceived. I don't think

much about it anymore; it's just the place
we lived a while years ago. There,
you hammered a toy cobbler's bench,

splashed in the cheap wading pool,
banked jumpers off a wobbly backboard,
shuffled out on your paper route.

I think much more about what I wanted
for you and worry if what I've provided
will prove to be what you needed

because soon you'll be in your own home,
and before long your brother will follow
with his own wife, his own life too,

which is why, if you ever wonder,
I sometimes call you in the middle of the day,
apparently for no particular reason.

Waltz at the Reception

—for Jim McLean

Everyone agreed the groom's dad would
have been less nervous at his own wedding.
He showed how difficult dancing is
with left feet planted in two worlds—
one as a father, one as a son. He planned
a waltz with his mother, *one,*
two, three, practiced the steps, *one*, two,
three, rehearsed their circuit around
and around and around and around
the scuffed parquet, *one*, two, three,
one, two, three. All offered prayers,
hoping his eager gesture would be found
pleasing. On the suddenly lonely floor precise
positions were assumed and music started,

and in the shapeable notes perhaps someone felt
at last the reliable beat that gives us measure:
time doesn't make our movements more sure;
we don't always do the right things well.
We learn to dance as we learn to walk—
uncertainly until we earn our rhythm,
until we share the melody of our spirit
and it becomes gift to us as we quarter turn
out of the box step, travelling forward,
forward into a twirl more graceful and unending
than the revolution of the earth.

Today's Game

—for Daniel and David

I umpire lazily, only occasionally
crouching over the game to make a disputed call.
The boys don't understand why
a liner through the picture window's an automatic out.
Explain that it's one of Doubleday's original ground rules,
and they miss the joke. But they've seen The Show;
they strut, spit, taunt their buddies, brush them back
high and tight, make a brilliant diving stop.
They can't yet make fine distinctions
outside the batter's box. They don't know what
the big deal is about careful. They don't care.
Whatever happens,
they won't mean it. They can't help it
that they've scrubbed an infield into the lawn.
My neighbor considers yard work a religious experience;
she looks across the hedge and agonizes
over my punished little acre
with a missionary's despair. She doesn't suffer
that fleeting thrill,
daring to steal second on your older brother,
propelled by joyous fear, sliding headfirst,
hugging the base just under your best friend's hard tag
in a thickening dusk dotted with fireflies.
                                    The teams change. Now
I'm out in right field, stabbing gracelessly
at my sons' stinging drives,
sliding myself, the taste of the dirt
wistful in my mouth as
they round their bases, sprinting away from me,
heading for home.
This short hot season ends too soon.
Even before we learn all the rules, we play it safe.
Just next week, we'll re-sow the grass.

Mama's Silver

—for Carol

Lift the lid of the handsome cherry chest, roll the hidden hinges.
Fine sterling rests in the slots where it has been stacked

for decades—knives, dinner forks, soup spoons, serving pieces.
Rub a finger over the velvety lining that soothes slight scratches

in bright metal. What does the soft luster of neatly ordered
handles and blades reflect? A shapely bride, middle child

of an earnest family, traveling by train one January across the South
to a military camp in Louisiana to marry her grinning airman,

revved up on the runway to war, who'd wrangled an overnight pass;
the festive meal welcoming a son home from the polio hospital;

an ailing grandfather's poignant birthday celebration; the first
visit with Mama and Daddy of a certain boyfriend, grinning himself,

head in his own clouds with love. Each piece knows a story,
each tine, each small smooth bowl, each edge muted too long

in a stepmother's hutch. Now, all are in a daughter's grateful hands
and can again do their natural work: spear a generous bite

of Company Mushroom Chicken, scoop a section of Men-Like-It Salad,
spread butter on Mema's Spoon Rolls, piping right out of the oven.

To the Young Man in Front of Me at Christmas Eve Vespers

—for Emmy Lou

The brush of your
grandmother's fingertips light
as idle snow

on your shoulder
never made you
turn your head. You should have

answered her gentle touch. I should have
leaned forward and tapped
the other shoulder. I should have

urged, *This night,*
of all nights, feel
the warmth of her gaze, see

the delight in her eyes.
I should have
because this is true:

with even an absent glance,
you would have known
how Mary approved of her baby.

Street Trade

Narrow woven bracelets dangle
by cheap clasps from an open umbrella,
imports displayed outside a sidewalk café.

Those at the margin of traffic are not
interrupted by this quiet commerce;
coffee continues to be sipped

out of silences in conversations,
gelato licked off waffle cones.
Some strollers pause to ask a price,

a few finger the finishes of the bands.
A skateboarder, Paige, she says,
a girl with long hair and longer legs,

examines the designs. She already wears
a similar loop, and buys another
in hues of mud and moss and milk.

From a case kept in a pack, beneath
clean socks and business permit,
the old peddler extracts a smoky bauble.

This highlights your eyes, he says, holding it
to the girl's ear. She accepts the glassy trinket
with a wide smile. The fine yarns flutter,

alive in the intermittent breezes
that wimple my wife's hair, pigments bright
as when blended from bark and berry,

earth and ash by poor village weavers
who carefully strung colored beads,
secured them with tiny knots.

On Seeing Bart Starr in the Nashville Airport

The wide concourse provided no more
cushion to hurrying passengers than Lambeau's
frozen tundra ever has to ball carriers beneath

a ton of tacklers, though nothing about this day's
swelter, as we waited to board for Cleveland, evoked
football until a familiar face emerged with others

arriving from Birmingham. The old quarterback
seemed as sure of his footing on the commercial
carpet as he did on icy scrabble under center,

time nearly gone. My sons, not much older
than I was one New Year's Eve when cars couldn't
start and whistles wouldn't blow and an excited

elderly fan died of exposure, would want to see him,
the younger would beg for an autograph. I waved
them back from buying candy and gum at a newsstand,

and they scooted to our gate, where I pointed out
the opportunity passing them by: A Hall of Famer
striding away, maybe a slight hitch in his step,

not quite swallowed by the crowd. The boys hustled
after him, cutting against the grain past stray
walkers, juking around those stopping,

staring at flight monitors. The smaller, speedier son's
run to daylight between two slow women helped him
hit paydirt. Almost. Almost close enough

to be touched yet eluding grasping fingers, the graying
athlete hesitated behind a stocky sales rep wheeling
a sample case across his path, then slashed through

a hole that closed as quickly as it opened, a nifty,
instinctive move that halted my son who raised his arms
overhead, signaling nothing more than frustration in failing

to reach his goal, no less surprised than journeyman
fullback Chuck Mercein, who, upon hearing *Brown right,*
31 wedge called in the frigid huddle, anticipated

a hero's moment, only to have the sneaky QB
keep the ball, dive into the endzone, deny him glory,
so he raised his own arms, avoiding a flag for pushing.

Atlantis Rising

STS-79 was launched from Kennedy Space Center at 4:54 a.m.,
September 16, 1996.

Hopeful pilgrims huddle by the dark sea, anxious for one brave ship,
and I crowd with them. At the edge of the known universe,

swirling salt breezes whisk our souls' deep waters
into choppy peaks that trace the current

rhythms of faithful hearts. We explore the enveloping night
like ancient, fretful land-lost sailors fingering sextants,

divining star charts, seeking another promising world,
until our patience receives its reward.

Beyond a far strip of shore where the surge laps and laps
survives an altar where Abraham might have struck his relative sacrifice.

Tonight, fresh flames flare there and soar, a precious new offering
accelerating through the dividing air. Then that fluid fire vanishes,

pursuing its own graceful geometry of arc and attitude,
while we stand still together there, gaping, grasping after

the holy wind that ignites the engine of imagination,
already circumnavigating the essential orbit of wonder.

Beth's Hands

Beth's hands on the keys never remind me of ivory-
tickling cliché. Not just clever fingers amused
with the naturals, the accidentals, the true thirds

spanning thumb and little finger, they are
instruments themselves, enjoying
deft inspirations released from a willing heart.

No discord diverts the compass of sound.
I watch Beth's hands moving over the octaves,
and when I listen to the music, they are what I hear.

In the Painter's Garden

—for Lynne

The scene below

the studio window is no tableau.
There is still life
there, still
in the garden corner where the nude was

posed and painted. Lush
hues. Shape and substance of
Eden. The familiar
face relieved by the heavy ivy
and the same current that today sails fern fronds
above the hanging baskets. Fluttering greenery
outlines the updraft that lifts to me
the gentle chatter, easy
laughter of a dozen

other guests. Listen.
Step over the dog, cross the deck.
Regard
the pieces on stretchers propped along the rail
and the framed collection exhibited on slender easels.
Consider how their characters change
as sunlight seeps through narrow fence slats,
slipping away across the weathered pavers, moss plump
among the fired stones. Tones darken, lines fade,
perceived depth deceives. Perhaps
another view, from another level
perhaps. You'll see. A discreet love has been made

here. Molecules from a sure heart mingled
with those of brush and brilliant palette and
seduced
the mysteries of color and light,
space and shadow,
into yielding
a connection with aspect and angle,
rapture and real risk, that passes
through us like the current between the Sistine fingers.

And there, still in the garden corner,
someone else's fingertips, delicate as moths,
dab another's forearm like an eager fan brush
feathering a primed and ready canvas.

Hope

—*for Mary T. Meagher Plant*

> *"The mastery of the turn is the story of our sky."*
> —William Langewiesche, *Inside the Sky*

Dip again into the racer's crouch,
toes rounded over the edge of the starting block—
a swallowtail poised on an azalea—
slick singlet a second skin, alert,
anticipating the launch from the perch.

You soared, lift derived
from strong shoulders and spirit,
with a fierce combustible grace in the fine air
imagined between layers of liquid.

Your flight plotted the fluid sine wave,
arm stroke and upsweep,
an undulating rhythm and roll
into the turn, the critical turn, one more
flip and dolphin kickout into one more
desperate pull through the hard water for one more
hundredth shaved from one more
bell lap.

Acolyte

—for Suzanne

In some congregations starched vestments solemnize
the ritual conduct of the light from narthex to nave,
but here a child brings in the flame simply
outfitted with a candlelighter and determination

to touch taper to wick, in no cassock or cotta.
Maybe it burdens juvenile arms to hoist and hold
the brass torch at angle to process up the aisle.
Maybe our call to worship will be delayed

by the steady trek toward the distant table
where a lone candle anticipates new fire.
No matter. The Lord said, "I am the light,"
and when we gather a child rekindles our belief.

One Sunday it may be a kindergartner in cowboy boots,
the next a third-grader in a tie-dyed tee
who delivers the symbol. The light holds their eyes.
The flicker they keep burning with deliberate steps

and a firm grip on the slender barrel conveys a spirit
beyond their current grasp. They don't know that
the splendor won't vanish if a hasty pace
overwhelms the height or heft of a quivering flame

or a shortened wick cannot claim a spark.
Another bulb will flare under a match,
a fresh candle will receive its holy kiss,
the radiance will consume all who welcome it.

All is as it has been and was meant to be.
The little shepherds do their helpful work—
bear the beacon to the altar, then snuff the candle
and return the light to the world. They don't see

on the faces they pass delighted smiles, gratitude
for such eager concentration applied to this ancient
task of transport, the acolyte in each one still
amazed by, still wondering at the light.

Wildflower Walk

—for Carol

At the bottom of Cedar Sink on a spring afternoon
the sky domes over our small hiking group,
a sphere of light and shadow, atmosphere and earth.
Breezes feather budding shoots and Bluets bow,

a quivering carpet off the path. Among the Trillium,
our guide points out the subtle perjury of flora,
the differences between True and False

Solomon's Seal. With a practiced hand, she gently lifts
a graceful arching stem, revealing tiny hanging blooms;
their absence, we learn, exposes the imposter variety.
There are other surprises here in the cool growth

where water flows from and back into the ground
and limestone slowly dissolves. We step over
fallen sycamores without worry for what

may be coiled against the unseen peeling bark.
Not taken so much with natural wonder,
I identify flowers as simple colors, a generic palette
in contrast to the relentless green—a red one here,

blue and yellow ones there—but our guide calls them
by their Christian names, delights in their personalities
—the showy pinkish sepals of Rue Anemone, airy

nodding spurs of Columbine, delicate lavender
hearts of Squirrel Corn, the floppy bells of Jacob's Ladder.
She's wandered these woods many times, and still
revels with a pilgrim's joy at each sighting of these

tender charms returned again after another bitter season,
eyes shining as clear as the heaven that envelops us,
impatient for us to be as amazed with these small miracles.

On Seeing the Van Goghs in Chicago

—for Ben, Carol, Claire, Claire, Daniel, Danny, Gail,
Jeanette, John, Martha, Marty, Melanie, Sherry & Whitney

For once, waiting in traffic didn't matter.
We enjoyed our leisure, eventually
taking in not only the yellow house in Arles,
but rowhouses on North Astor and coffeehouses on Rush.
Remember the unforced pace of days
achieving lift from the collective spirit
with which we answered the persistent wind,
always in our faces. We rose on its gusts
like a wedge of geese against the vault of heaven,
in which Jesus assured us there are many mansions.
He could've said that even in the slums of Providence
there are luxuries that exceed our grace, pleasures
enough to make us sing, a gospel choir, standing
unrobed in the doorways to our rooms.

ACKNOWLEDGEMENTS

Thanks to the editors who first published these poems, sometimes in slightly different form, in the following journals and anthologies: "A Matter of Public Record" in the chapbook *Absent Photographer*; "Acolyte," *Fathom Magazine;* "At the Game Preserve," *Jelly Bucket;* "Atlantis Rising," *Exposition Review*; "Before Mammoth Cave," *Kentucky Monthly*; "Beth's Hands," in the anthology *Motif^V1: Writing by Ear*; "Burned," *Amethyst Review*; "Called Out," *Amethyst Review*; "Common Stock," in the anthology *Motif^V2: Come What May;* "Cycle," *The Heartland Review* and *Main Channel Voices;* "Down Home," *Journal of Kentucky Studies*; "Dream House," *Vitamin ZZZ;* "Dying," *Branchwood Journal;* "Easing Out the Clutch," *Capsule Stories;* "Faith," *ProCreation;* "Hard Hat," *Cadenza*; "Hippos Humping," *Cape Magazine;* "Hope," *Inkwell;* "In Memoriam," *Seminary Ridge Review*; "In the Driveway," *The Heartland Review*; "In the Painter's Garden," *Wind;* "Juleps on the Reading Porch," *Kentucky Monthly*; "Mama's Silver," in the anthology *Heat the Grease, We're Frying Up Some Poetry*; "Mourners Leaned Against Their Cars," *Headline Poetry & Press*; "My Albanian Nurse," *Better Than Starbucks*; "My Broken Heart," *Pegasus;* "My EKG," *Hospital Drive*; "My Father's Socks," *Main Channel Voices*; "Near the Border," *Pegasus*; "On Seeing Bart Starr in the Nashville Airport," *Aethlon: The Journal of Sport Literature;* "On Seeing the Van Goghs in Chicago," *Cæsura*; "Performance Leadership," *Cape Magazine*; "Photo from My Sister's Wedding," *Cape Magazine;* "Sitting Behind Seven Women," *The Heartland Review*; "Statues in an Antique Store," *Cape Magazine;* "Street Trade," *The Walled City Literary Review;* "Tasseled Loafers," *The Writers' Café Magazine;* "The Night Room," *Hospital Drive;* "This Afternoon in London," *Poetry and Places;* "Tipping Point," *River & South Review*; "To a Little Girl Considering a Snapping Turtle on Spring Branch," *Off the Coast*; "To My Older Son, Soon to Marry," *The Heartland Review*; "To the Young Man in Front of Me at Christmas Eve Vespers," *Branchwood Journal*; "Today's Game," *Fan: A Baseball Literary Magazine;* "Tool," *N.C. Bards—Greensboro Winston-Salem Review;* "Waltz at the Reception," *Halfway Down the Stairs*; "Wedding Party," *The Raven Review;* "Wildflower Walk," *Jelly Bucket*.

"In the Driveway" won the 2003 Joy Bale Boone Poetry Award.

"Wildflower Walk" won the 2017 George Scarbrough Poetry Prize.

"Burned" will be included in the anthology *Without a Doubt: poems illuminating faith*, to be published by NYQ Books, the New York Quarterly Foundation, 2022.

"Waltz at the Reception" was nominated for Best of the Net, 2021.

THANK YOU

How many chances do you get to thank those who helped or influenced your journey as a poet and writer? This might be it. So, I'm taking full advantage of the opportunity.

Thanks to my nearly lifelong friend Susan Webster Vallance. Over half a century ago she said or did something—who knows now what—that caused me to start writing.

Thanks to the late Priscilla Adams and to Gayle Manahan. Ms. Adams was my first creative writing teacher, at Grimsley High School in Greensboro, North Carolina. She gave me an "A-" on the first piece I wrote in her class, which made it easier to keep trying. Rejection may be part of a writer's life, but acceptance in any form, especially early on, is a powerful motivator. Ms. Manahan was my senior English teacher. She made English fun. I became an English major in college partly because of her.

At Mars Hill College I was blessed to have Dr. Pat Verhulst as my advisor, teacher and friend. She's the other reason I became an English major. For four years she encouraged and critiqued my writing and made sure I didn't settle. My Mars Hill classmates Ken Chamlee and the late Linda Davis March are among the best poets I've known. At an important time, they set the standard to which I aspired. Thanks!

The late Kentucky Poet Laureate Joy Bale Boone was a dear friend and mentor for many years. This book is dedicated to her memory. Along with Joy, Western Kentucky University English Professor Emeritus Loretta Martin Murrey founded the Rain Stick Poets, a writing group that met monthly for six years, until Joy's passing, and then somewhat less regularly for over nine years afterwards. Quite a few of the poems in this collection were workshopped by and improved with the help of the Rain Sticks. Joy, Loretta and Natalie Lund, Bonnie Meyer, David Rogers, Billy Vincent, and the late Liz Lapinski were a challenging and supportive group. I appreciate them all. Bonnie, Loretta and Natalie were early readers of this collection; their comments and suggestions improved it.

Thanks to all at the Mountain Heritage Literary Festival at Lincoln Memorial University in Harrogate, Tennessee. For more than a dozen years, the MHLF has been an annual writing home away from home. I've made wonderful friends there and learned from outstanding poets and writers. Several deserve special mention: Darnell Arnoult, Joseph Bathanti, Katy Giebenhain, Thomas Alan Holmes, Denton Loving, Maurice Manning, Lisa Parker and Larry Thacker. (An extra measure of appreciation goes to Joseph and Maurice.)

I've benefited over the years from relationships with exceptional talents in disciplines other than poetry. Three decades ago, Mary Weaver, then the editor at *Storytelling Magazine*, gave me my first opportunity as a "professional" writer; her skill as an editor greatly improved the articles I wrote for her and my ability as a writer. At Horse Cave (Ky.) Theatre, Director Warren Hammack's playwriting workshops exposed me to a different writing world—and led to one of the best experiences of my life. Thanks a million to Warren and fellow playwrights Liz Bussey Fentress, Nancy Gall-Clayton, EK Larken (a.k.a. Scout Link), Walter May, and the late Temple Dickinson.

Thanks to Ron Carlson; my sister, Bryn Chapman; my friends Shelby Bale, Rich Alexander, and Randy Yocum; and to Hart County's favorite son and former Mammoth Cave guide Davis McCombs.

Thanks to Leah, Christen, Kevin, Jennifer, Jackie and the rest of the great team at Finishing Line Press. I was thrilled when they accepted my manuscript. It's been a pleasure to work with them during the production process.

Of course, I wouldn't be here without my parents, Lawrence and Gerry Pike, and I'm sure I wouldn't be *here*, either, the author of this collection, if they hadn't encouraged reading and learning from an early age. Lots of 12-year-old boys had subscriptions to *Boys Life*, and many probably also got *Sports Illustrated* too. I may have been the only one in my hometown, though, who also had his own subscriptions to *The Atlantic, Harper's* and *Esquire*. Thanks, Mom and Dad, for that and so much more.

Thanks to my daughter-in-law, Amy, and granddaughters, Anne Rhoades and Emaline, for adding a dimension to life I never imagined while raising two sons. There's truth in the old saying: If I'd known grandchildren were this much fun, I would have had them first.

Finally, and most of all, thanks to my wife, Carol, and sons, Daniel and David. They inspired some of the poems in this volume; all reflect their support and encouragement. They have always believed in me. What a gift!

Glasgow, Kentucky
October 2021

Larry Pike's poetry and fiction has appeared in *The Louisville Review, Seminary Ridge Review, Cæsura, Exposition Review, Cadenza, Capsule Stories, Jelly Bucket,* several anthologies, and other publications. His play *Beating the Varsity* was the "Kentucky Voices" production at Horse Cave (Ky.) Theatre in 2000, and it was published in *World Premieres from Horse Cave Theatre* (Motes Books, 2009); two other plays have received staged readings. He is a graduate of Mars Hill College (B.A., English) and Purdue University (M.A., communication). A retired human resources manager, he worked for the same company for over forty-two years. He lives with his wife, Carol, in Glasgow, Kentucky. This is his first collection of poetry.